SOUTH AFRICA
IN TRANSITION

SOUTH AFRICA

Cape
Town
TABLE
BAY
DEVILS
PEAK
TABLE MT.
CAPE PENINSULA
CAPE OF
GOOD
HOPE
Atlantic Ocean

KRUGER

NATIONAL

PARK

TRANSVAAL

Pretoria

Johannesburg

WITWATERS RAND

Vereeniging

SWAZILAND

ORANGE
FREE STATE

ZULULAND

NATAL

KALAHARI

DESERT

Kimberley

Bloemfontein

BASUTOLAND

INANDA

Pietermaritzburg

Durban

ORANGE R.

NAMAQUALAND

Atlantic Ocean

CAPE PROVINCE

ORANGE R.

DRAKENSBERG

Indian Ocean

Vanderbyl

TRANSKEI

GREAT KARROO

ZWARTBERG

LITTLE KARROO

Paarl

Cape Town

Stellenbosch

CAPE
OF GOOD HOPE

Ocean

AFRICA

Atlantic
Ocean

SOUTH
AFRICA

Indian
Ocean

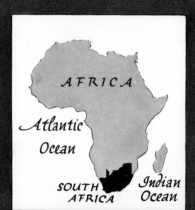

0   50   100 Miles

palacios

look to a day when no skill, no knowledge, no occupation, and therefore no right and no responsibility, will be closed to Africans.

One thing is certain. Such a day is coming. How long it will take, no one can say. Meanwhile, here is this record of one of the stages of the journey. To understand that journey fully, it is necessary to know a little of our history, and this I shall try to present as objectively and honestly as I can; but the very brevity of the account is a limiting factor.

A BRIEF HISTORY

THE Dutch first came to the Cape of Good Hope in 1652, under the command of Jan van Riebeeck. The intention was not to establish a colony, but merely a refreshment station on the long voyage between Holland and Batavia. Yet their more adventurous spirits began to move away from the shelter of Table Mountain and the comforts of Cape Town, first into that majestic mountain country that is the chief characteristic and glory of this part of Africa. Eventually these adventurers, or their sons, reached these harsh regions known as the Little and the Great Karroo, a country very different from the southernmost parts of the subcontinent, and as different from Holland as any could be. There was no one to contest their early passage but the Hottentots and the Bushmen. Some of the Hottentots adapted themselves in a fashion to the new state of affairs; they entered into the service of the Dutch townsmen and farmers, and constituted an important element in the make-up of the emerging Cape Colored People. The Bushmen, a wandering race, small in stature, hardy as the Karroo itself, deadly hunters with poisoned arrows, retreated into mountain caves and desert, and today only a protected remnant survives in the dry Kalahari.

The northward, north-eastward, and eastward advance of the trekkers, spreading like a fan from Cape Town was relatively uncontested in the more central portions of the Cape, but it encountered, in the 1770's, in the more eastward and coastal regions, the fierce opposition of a warlike African people known as the Xhosas. They, like the trekkers, were cattle-owners, and a bitter frontier struggle ensued. It was here that the doctrine of *apartheid*, that is racial separateness, though it was not yet called by that name, became firmly established. Only in *apartheid* could the trekker see any hope for his survival in this hard and dangerous continent. The feeling against racial intermixture, already strong, hardened; only two relationships were permissible between white and black, the relationship of master and servant, or the relationship of enemy and enemy. Any equality was utterly repellent; above all, there was to be no sexual commerce whatever, in marriage or out of it.

Such conditions of isolation and danger might have led to the degeneration of the trekkers, but religion exercised a powerful influence over them. The Bible was their constant companion, and in particular they were attracted by the stories of the patriarchs, which seemed so relevant to their hard and lonely life. Who indeed could have been nearer to the patriarchs than they themselves, as they moved or sojourned in the wilderness with their flocks and herds, their menservants and maidservants, with a determination to be faithful and survive?

Their Dutch language, already changing, continued to change in a fascinating way, becoming much simplified, and enriching itself with a host of new idioms influenced by the kind of country they lived in and the kind of life they led, by the ox, the waggon, the loneliness, the dry watercourse and the thorn. To this country they gave a fierce possessive love. Their new language they eventually called Afrikaans, the language of Africa; and they eventually called themselves the Afrikaners, the people of Africa. They had indeed grown far from Holland, and from the Dutch East India Company, now in its decline.

Now, in the very early 1800's, a new and powerful factor entered into the situation. During the Napoleonic wars, the British took over the Cape. They were in the main administrators, but in their wake came missionaries preaching brotherhood and equality, and in 1820 the first group of British settlers. As a result of British zeal, the slaves were emancipated. In the frontier wars the British authorities supported sometimes the trekkers, sometimes the Xhosas. They sent a white officer with Hottentot soldiers to arrest a white farmer, who resisted and was killed; his friends rebelled, and five were hanged at Slagter's Nek in 1815, one of the bitter events of what was to be called the Century of Wrong.

Then came the Great Trek of 1836, a search for a new country where there was no government but one's own, and where the doctrines of *apartheid* could be carried out in purity. Yielding the search for a passage along the eastern coasts, the trekkers turned northeast, crossed the Orange River, and reached the central plateau of the interior, where they founded the Boer republics of the Orange Free State and the Transvaal, in the latter of which there was to be "no equality in church or state". After a brief occupation of Natal on the east coast, where British traders had first arrived in 1824, the trekkers were expelled, and returned to the interior, where they hoped they would now be left alone.

Their hope was not fulfilled. On the other side of the Orange River, all unknown, lay a wealth of gold and diamonds such as the world had not known before. It was the discovery of gold in the Transvaal, in 1886, that proved catastrophic. Fortune-seekers, many of them British, streamed into the Republic, eventually demanding some say in Government, which President Kruger felt that it would be fatal to concede, arguing that this would mean the end of all for which the Afrikaner had fought, suffered, and died. Down in the Cape was the Prime Minister, Cecil Rhodes, dreaming of an all-British route from the Cape to Cairo, dreaming of how a man could change the world if he had enough money and enough power. And after Rhodes's downfall, Milner, cold and resolute. So in 1899 came the climactic event of the Century of Wrong, the Anglo-Boer War. Few Britishers would defend it now, but it is only the South Africans who know that it is still being paid for today.

The victory of the British in 1902; their restoration of self-government within the British Empire to the defeated republics in 1906; the astonishing coming together of the Cape, Free State, Transvaal, and Natal, in the new Union of South Africa in 1910; the great talk of peace and reconciliation; these events concealed for a while the real course of events. Magnanimity does not heal the wounds of war. In 1912 was formed the Afrikaner Nationalist Party, pledged to the achievement of republican independence for South Africa, and a return to the doctrines of *apartheid*.

The early governments of the Union of South Africa were essentially governments of partnership between the two white races; reconciliation was the keynote of political policy. But Nationalism, fostered by powerful cultural organisations, and strengthened by the growing separation of the two white races in school and university, finally triumphed under Dr. Malan in 1948. Neither in Dr. Malan's Cabinet nor in the present Cabinet of Mr. Strijdom is there any English-speaking Minister. Legislation from 1948 till today has had one supreme purpose, and that is to translate *apartheid* into law, and to ensure that the future development of South Africa shall forever be in accordance with the custom and doctrine of racial separation, as completely as can be achieved. Two points should be made here. The Government, though in a commanding majority in Parliament owing to certain electoral provisions favouring rural districts, and to its own creation of a Senate in which it has 77 out of 89 seats, secured at the last election roughly half of the votes. Now as the white population is slightly more than 60% Afrikaans-speaking, and slightly less than 40% English-speaking, it will be seen that the political divisions are not absolutely coincident with racial divisions. Shall we put it this way, that the Nationalists are overwhelmingly Afrikaans-speaking, and the English-speaking people are overwhelmingly in the opposition?

The second point is this. The opposition is not markedly different from the Government in its race attitudes. Their objections to *apartheid* are practical rather than moral, though they undoubtedly feel what could be described as moral uneasiness.

Is modern industrialism compatible with *apartheid*? Will the Government allow development to proceed unchecked, or will they divert part of it (and it will have to be a large part) to the tribal reserves, and so reverse the stream to the cities? Can the white people of South Africa enjoy a high standard of living, unless the African people are fully drawn into its industrial revolution? Can one draw people fully in, and deny them political rights?

It is no part of our intention to answer these questions here, except to point out that the very difficulty of them causes even amongst the Afrikaner Nationalists a sharp difference of opinion, some calling for complete territorial separation of races, others arguing that Africans who enter industry in white areas must understand fully that in those areas they cannot expect the freedom which is promised to them in their own reserves; they cannot own land, or move freely or enter certain occupations. Nor must they expect, in these areas or any other, to exercise the Parliamentary vote, for this would mean, according to Mr. Strijdom, the end of white civilization. In the meantime, the industrial revolution is considerably advanced, and many of these photographs show clearly the joys and sorrows, the changing habits of dress, and the vitality of the people most affected by it. Most of these illustrations are drawn from Johannesburg, which is at it should be.

It is fascinating to reflect, that just as Johannesburg and Pretoria once controlled the destiny of the Transvaal, they now control the destiny of South Africa. In 1899 it was Johannesburg that threatened to conquer Pretoria; in 1956 the contrary is true.

These two cities stand, not quite for Rhodes and Kruger, not quite for Gold and Religion, not quite for Opposition and Government, not quite for Democracy and Autocracy; and the reader will understand that when I say "not quite", I also mean "not quite not". They stand for two conflicting strains in South African life, neither of which has ever triumphed.

But now a third element is entering the situation. Of its vigor and vitality, of its power to laugh in squalor, of its hunger to participate fully in man's new world, in respect of both its rewards and its obligations, these photographs do not leave one in doubt.

THE PHYSICAL COUNTRY

IT must be clear from this story that there is no one thing that South Africa means to all its peoples, as, for example, the United States does to hers. There can in fact be only one common patriotism, and that is to the physical land in which we live; and even then we are able to invest a mountain with political emotion.

South Africa is of great physical beauty. It is a raised plateau, falling east, south, and west to the sea, the whole country being set between the Atlantic and Indian oceans, which situation, combined with its elevatedness, gives to it a climate as equable as any in the world. The drop on the east is spectacular; the escarpment of the Drakensberg, which reaches in places an altitude of 10,000 feet, must fall in a hundred miles to the shores of the Indian Ocean, which it does in a scenic confusion of hills, valleys and rivers, called Natal. The higher parts of this province are verdant and grass-covered, the lower parts wooded and sub-tropical, with a wealth of fruit and flower, earning for it the name of the Garden Province.

Behind the escarpment lie the interior provinces of the Orange Free State and the Transvaal, the old Boer republics. The Free State is a featureless and treeless plain, but in that part of the Transvaal which lies to the east of the escarpment, the country is very like the Garden Province in scenery and fertility.

The fourth province of the Union of South Africa is the Cape of Good Hope. By common consent it is the southernmost part, culminating in the Cape Peninsula and its Table Mountain, which is one of the most majestic parts of all South Africa. But this grandeur is by no means confined to the south; the mountain passes through and over the three parallel ranges of the Cape Province are amongst the scenic glories of the country. The first of these ranges intercepts most successfully the moisture-laden winds from the sea, and the coastal region is wooded and fertile. Behind the first range lies the little Karroo, a dry, stony, and altogether fascinating region, which with the rains bursts out into a blaze of purple and yellow. And behind the second lies the arid Great Karroo, whose beauty is only for the connoisseur.

Is there anything in North America that looks like South Africa? Yes, Texas, Arizona, Utah, bear some resemblance to the interior plain. Florida, while resembling Natal in climate, has none of its tumbled panoramas. Natal is as unlike anything in North America as the wooded hills and valleys of Connecticut are unlike anything in South Africa. Our forests—and there is not much of them—run like fingers into the southward-facing kloofs that catch the wet ocean winds. South African scenery is wide and sweeping, set under a wide and sweeping sky. Its beauty is vast, not local and immediate, a matter of light and color and distance, not of field and stream and tree. Anything less like the beauties of Britain, Holland, France and Germany, from which countries most of our settlers came, could hardly be imagined.

THE PHOTOGRAPHS

THE first picture following this text is of a group of African men, who, after a period of work on the gold mines are returning to the tribal reserves. The pictures following give some impression of the kind of places to which they are returning. About four million people live in the reserves, and though much of this land is good, the pressure upon it is very heavy. Extensive areas are badly eroded, and although the authorities are making great efforts to combat it, the very nature of the terrain, the pressure of population, and the lack of farming skill, make it unlikely that the reserves will ever provide anything but a poor life.

For the traveller the reserves are fascinating, especially in those parts where tribal tradition is still relatively strong, and where tribal dress is still worn. The reserves themselves are in transition; where they are situated near a city, they are almost entirely dependent on it. But this dependence is less noticeable in the larger and more remote reserves, of which Zululand and the Transkei are two notable examples.

On the next six pages the pictures are as follows:

1. African miners leaving Johannesburg for the reserves.

2. The wide rolling country of the Transkei, larges of all the reserves.

3. The mountain country of Swaziland.

4. Xhosa mother and child.

3

4

5

5 & 6.   This is a part of a tribal reserve, not many miles from the city of Durban in Natal. The small boy with the stick is the herdsman, and must see that the cattle do not stray into the fields. The Umgeni River runs through the reserve, and women wash their clothes on the banks. The scenery is magnificent, the vegetation luxuriant, the summer hot, the winter perfect. Most of the men of this district work in Durban, in factories, shops, and domestic service, returning home for the weekends. This scene is situated in the famous Valley of a Thousand Hills.

6

7

7 & 8.   Kraal in Zululand.

8

9. Ndebele woman outside her house.

NATAL

NATAL is that part of South Africa that lies under the highest part of the Drakensberg escarpment. It is, in respect of its white inhabitants, the most British of the four provinces; however, the great majority of its people are Zulu-speaking. Durban is called the most English city, and so it is; but it is exciting because its streets are alive with the sights and sounds and voices of Europe and Africa and the East, all of this set in a scene of such natural luxuriance and colour as I do not remember to have seen surpassed by any other city of the world.

The coastal hills, once covered with low forest, are now largely given over to waving sugar-cane plantations. Tropical fruits grow in great abundance, pineapples, bananas, litchis, avocados, guavas, granadillas, mangos, and pawpaws. Flowering plants and shrubs and trees are equally abundant. In October and November, in Durban and Pietermaritzburg and many other towns, the jacarandas put out a wealth of mauve blossoms, which, fallen, carpet the streets below. In January in Durban the flat crowns of the flamboyants, noble trees in any season, are covered with scarlet flowers, while the spathodea, the African Flame, bears its large orange blooms almost the whole year round. The winter months are even more prodigal. While the interior plain burns brown and lifeless, here bougainvilleas cascade down from the houses, and the Golden Shower, bignonia venusta, covers roofs and walls in sheets of orange flame. The kaffirboom, erythrina caffra, puts forth its blood-red clusters and the poinsettias their scarlet bracts. Another striking bush is the acacia floribunda with its profusion of yellow flowers. A few miles inland from Durban, where the hills begin to rise sharply, the gardens in September and October are magnificent with flowering azaleas. Natal is justly called the Garden Province.

Durban is a city of more than a half-a-million people, of whom roughly one third are white, one third Zulu or Zulu-speaking, and one third Indians. It is one of the busiest ports of the whole continent, and is a thriving center of industry, possessing many splendid modern buildings.

Most of the white citizens of Durban live on the magnificent hill known as the Berea, which begins to rise a mile or two from the beaches, affording a cooler air and magnificent views of ocean and harbor. Its residential streets are planted with the flamboyant, jacaranda and spathodea; and these and many noble indigenous trees excite the admiration of almost every visitor.

Its main shopping thoroughfare is West Street, but one block to the north of this is the Indian city. When Indian laborers were brought to Natal, they were followed by traders, mostly Muslims, some of whom succeeded in establishing notable businesses. No visitor must neglect to visit this portion of the city. Here are shops displaying exquisite silks and Oriental jewellery, and others out of whose doors come the mingled fragrances of all the spices of the East. Here also are temples, mosques, and churches; and the Indian market, one of the sights of the city.

In the streets will be seen people of all races. Though young Indian girls usually wear European dress, when they are grown up they return to the sari, whose bright colors are to be seen on every hand. Many Muslim men wear the fez, and occasionally—but now a rare sight—may be seen some old humble man who wears the traditional clothes of the lowly laborer. Many Europeans will be seen also, mostly women out shopping. But the most striking sight will be Zulu women in tribal dress; they have probably come considerable distances to visit their husbands in Durban, and they cannot but attract attention when they walk unconcernedly through the streets of this twentieth-century city.

Two of the pictures in this section were taken at a Shembe wedding, a few miles from Durban. The Shembeites are a Christian sect, but their founder sought to retain for Christianity much of Zulu custom and of that vivid ceremony and dance which is of such deep significance in African life. The whole wedding ceremony, totally unlike its counterpart in the conventional church, is accompanied by dancing, singing and the rhythmical clapping of hands. The bride appears contemptuous of the gifts humbly displayed to her, and finally runs away, only to be recaptured. While she evinces this unwillingness, the bridegroom shows hurt and shame, awakening in the unversed spectator sympathetic feelings of distress.

This dancing took place in the Inanda hills on a summer afternoon. But Mr. Weiner was also able to photograph dancing at Cato Manor, one of the worst slums of the city. He was at first treated with coldness and hostility, but the fact that he was accompanied by an African friend, coupled, I regret to say, with the discovery that he was not a South African, melted the resistance, and he was treated to dancing of tremendous gusto.

10

10 & 11.   Only one block to the north of Durban's shopping center, begins another world. Most of its shops are owned by Indians, and many of its customers are Africans, some from the remoter districts of Natal. These two pictures show this part of Durban. In the first, the two men are workers in the city, the two women are visitors from the tribal reserves. The woman on the left wears a handkerchief over her breasts as a concession to convention.

The young man in the second picture is not a city worker. His strange manner of dress indicates both an acceptance and a rejection of city ways. These are the city clothes of thousands of young tribesmen like himself, and in Durban they attract no attention.

12

12 & 13.   At the Shembe wedding. The third man from the left, with shield, is the bridegroom. Occupying the stage is a clowning woman. With an imaginary fountain pen she will soon write out the marriage certificate, and assuming the haughty benevolence she thinks appropriate to a white official, she will offer the certificate to the bridegroom. Below her, another woman reassembles the gifts that the bride has scorned.

On the right are the bride and her attendant, who carries an umbrella, an article that time has declared to be congruous with tribal dress.

14. In Cato Manor a Zulu woman diviner dances, to singing and clapping of hands; all this a few miles from Durban City Hall.

14

15

15. Here has been captured the vigor and vitality of a South African slum in its happier moments. The two dancers are utterly absorbed, and if they have anxieties and frustrations, this is not the time to remember them. Just how to give fuller expression to this vitality is one of the supreme political problems of the country.

16

16, 17 & 18.   More scenes from the streets of Durban, again showing tribal people in the city. The African portrayed on the upper right in striking regalia is a ricksha puller; this is a dying occupation, kept alive by holiday-makers and sightseers from abroad. Observe the three newspaper sellers, standing under a name plate in Afrikaans, with papers and magazines in one or other of our two official languages.

17

18

19

19. What is this small boy doing here in the market, when he should be in school? He is watching an Indian fruitseller's baskets, and will earn a few pence for it. He does not know where his mother is, and his father he has never seen at all. His future is only too easy to foretell.

20. Two crippled African women buying bread at a stall. The crippled African child of today has a much greater chance of receiving remedial treatment.

21 & 22.   Much of the flower and vegetable trade of Natal is in the hands of Indians, both as growers and sellers. Here is seen an Indian woman returning from the market with a sack of potatoes, which she will now retail in small lots; she herself lives in a place too small for the growing of crops, but she has clung to the kind of life she understands best. The poorer Indian people were renowned for their gardening skill, and their humble industry; the whole family took part in the cultivation of the family plot. Now many of them are city people, facing the future with anxiety and uncertainty, but not without courage.

23

24

23. A group of Indian children, sitting before a bench on which is the family ritual brass, out for a cleaning. All these children except the youngest are at school, the Province of Natal having, with the aid of the Indian people themselves, made better and better provision for their education. But what are they to do after that? That is the great question. Many occupations are closed to them, and because of this, many of their best students have become teachers, so that Indian teachers are among the best qualified in South Africa.

24. Indian basket-makers.

25.   A family at Merebank, Durban.

CAPE TOWN

CAPE TOWN is our Mother city. She lies under the wall of Table Mountain, that stands 3600 feet out of Table Bay. To live in this part of South Africa, which is called the Cape Peninsula, is to live always in the sight of and under the shadow of some mountain. The drive from the city to the tip of the peninsula is one of the most spectacular in Africa. The mountains fall straight into the sea, and the road runs high above the ocean, under the peaks known as the Twelve Apostles. Then it descends, and runs along a lonely and beautiful tongue of land to the lighthouse at Cape Point. Here you look out to the South Pole, with the Atlantic on your left, and the Indian Ocean on your right. These ships that you see here have three world routes open to them, to London via the Suez Canal, to India and the far East via Mombasa, or to Australia and New Zealand via no landfall at all.

Here in Cape Town are to be seen examples of the most stately forms of domestic architecture that man has devised. Its striking characteristics are the Dutch gables, the whitewashed walls, the spacious and lofty interiors, the massive furniture, the long stoeps shaded by the oaks. These houses rejoice in names like Vergelegen, Rhine, Meerlust, Groot Constantia, Perel Vallei, Stellenberg, and Alphen. They are not all on the Peninsula, some being found in that equally magnificent mountain country adjoining Cape Town. Groot Constantia is easily reached: it was built in 1685, and after being destroyed by fire, was faithfully rebuilt by the Union Government and is open to visitors.

The Cape Peninsula is rich in memories of Cecil Rhodes, fateful genius of the sub-continent in the latter part of the nineteenth century. He came out from England to die, but lived enormously instead. He liked big things, especially big events; he became Prime Minister of the Cape of Good Hope, controlled the diamonds of Kimberley, exercised a powerful and dangerous influence in Johannesburg, gave his name to a town and a university, and finally to two countries. He dreamed of the all-British route from the Cape to Cairo, founded the Rhodes Scholarhips, and had himself buried on top of a granite hill called World's View, in Southern Rhodesia.

He was a great man, of the Napoleonic rather than the Lincolnian kind, corrupted by power and dreams of power. His ends may have been big, but he was careless about means. When Kruger opposed him, he knew no solution except in terms of power. When his friend Leander Starr Jameson led his raid from Rhodesia, against the Transvaal in 1895, and failed, Rhodes's day was done. If the Boer War was the great dividing event of our history, Rhodes was the great dividing personality; ironically, his aim was to unite.

Under the mountain stands his Memorial and the magnificent house called Groote Schuur which he bequeathed to the Prime Ministers of the unborn country of South Africa; also the handsome buildings of the University of Cape Town, one of the finest in the country.

One of the sights of Cape Town are the stands of the Cape Colored flower sellers. Some sell their wares in front of the General Post Office, and some behind it on the Square in September and October. The color and variety of these flowers are wide-ranging, for this is the southern spring, and the mountains and valleys of the Cape of Good Hope, not only near Cape Town but for hundreds of miles along the eastern coasts, are covered with a diversity of wild flowers unsurpassed by any comparable region in the world. There are disas, watsonias and gladioli, and numerous heaths from the mountainsides; the vleis are white with arum lilies; but most striking of all are the proteas, of all kinds and sizes, the flower appearing outwardly to be a cup of leaves, which changes from external green to the most delicate of colors, the whole enclosing a most attractive bloom. The protea is one of the national emblems of our country, ranking in this category with the delicate antelope called the springbok.

It is not only Cape Town nor the Cape Peninsula that is the holiday maker's para-dise. If we travel across the Cape Flats, the sandy and uninteresting tract that separates peninsula from continent, we enter an entrancing country, the land of Stellenbosch and Paarl and the Drakenstein Valley, of the old Dutch houses and the oaks and the vineyards. Every place we visit is under a mountain, every mountain is full of streams; small wonder that South Africans speak wistfully about the Cape. There is everything there, mountains, streams, fruits and flowers, white gabled houses and museums and galleries; people say there is history here, although we don't lack history in other places. The truth is, it is a relatively gracious and urbane history, without that fierceness that characterises the rest of us. Yet there is a reminder of this larger world in the Parliament that assembles every January at the top of Adderley Street, and makes fierce and iron laws.

26

26. "The fairest Cape in the whole circumference of the earth"—Sir Francis Drake

Flanked by Devil's Peak and Lion's Head, this is the famous Table Mountain, beneath which lies the city of Cape Town, and the harbor of Table Bay.

27. The Flower Sellers.

28

28. Cape Colored carrot pickers on the way to market.

29. A small old Dutch house, dating from 1797, in the University town of Stellenbosch. The thatched roof has now yielded to corrugated iron, discolored and corroded.

29

30. A Cape Colored burial place.

31

31 & 32.   The Dutch gable, the white walls, the thatched roof, the oaks—an old Cape house set in the majestic mountain country of the Cape of Good Hope. There is nothing else like this in Africa, nor indeed anywhere in the world.

32

33

33. Cape Colored boy and girl.

34. The old Malay Quarter of Cape Town.

34

35. The Industrial Revolution always does this. But we always hope that it also promises something better. It sometimes takes a long time.

36

36 & 37. Cape Colored Pensioners, awaiting the monthly payment. In these pictures are to be seen clearly—or so I fancy—all the racial strains which have gone to make the Cape Colored People.

37

THE PEOPLES
OF SOUTH AFRICA

THE first white men who left the security of Cape Town and the Peninsula, and moved out north and north-east and east into unknown country, were hardy, brave and independent. The terrain into which they moved was varied. Some of it was beautiful and fertile, lending itself to permanent settlement. But some of it was harsh and arid, the great expanses of the interior plain. Here were to be found the trek-boers, and it was amongst them that the wandering spirit was strongest. Their farms were of tremendous extent, and as they multiplied, their children moved further and further into the interior. Europe, and the life of Europe, ceased to have great meaning for them, and they gave their undivided love to this part of Africa to which destiny had led them. It is indeed a reproach often levelled by their descendants against the English-speaking people of South Africa, that they are still British in their outlook and have never fully accepted their new country as their home.

This reproach has today lost a great deal of its force. The practice of referring to England or Britain as "home" is almost dead; amongst my own English-speaking friends I do not know one who does it. But it is true, I think, that the English-speaking South African is more European than is the Afrikaner. This happens for several reasons. He has always been largely a town-dweller and feels less remote from the outside world; many of the interests which concern him have links with similar interests in other countries; his books—though this is changing—are to a great extent published in overseas countries; his commercial and industrial undertakings, his churches, and even his schools and universities, have these same origins and connections. Most of all, perhaps, he wants, both with head and heart, South Africa to belong to the British Commonwealth of Nations, and to acknowledge the British Crown. Whatever his intellectual reasons for this, he has two emotional ones, the first historical and readily comprehensible, the second because of his fear of Afrikaner Nationalism and its exclusiveness.

We are therefore, all of us, people in transition, and it is South Africa that is doing this to us. The black African people are having their lives changed beyond recognition by an industrial society; the Indian people are becoming more and more Europeanised in thought and custom, though Eastern religions are still powerful; the English-speaking people are becoming more and more South African in outlook; the

Cape Colored People are, like the African, being drawn more and more into the industrial society.

The Afrikaner people themselves are by no means immune to these forces. They became, by reason of their trek into the interior, a largely rural and farming people, and indeed were at one time called the Boers, that is, the farmers. Though they still often use this word amongst themselves, it would now be impolite for another person to do so. But today the Afrikaner people are also becoming an urban people. Their schools and universities are of the highest standard, and their public men have a command of the two official languages which surpasses that of the great majority of English-speaking South Africans. Their business men have entered the fields of banking, commerce, and industry, but it will be some time before they reach a position of equality. However they are all-powerful in the field of government, both in regard to legislation and administration; they are in the majority, sometimes overwhelmingly, in the Civil Service, the Postal Services, the South African Railways, and the South African Police. All this has had the effect of bringing more and more Afrikaners to the cities, and has also brought the two white races into association throughout the entire country. There is no tendency, as in Canada, for the two races to remain geographically separate.

Something should be said about the nature of this association between the white races. The schools, universities, churches, and cultural organisations are quite separate; on the other hand, there is no separation in cinema, theatre, residential suburb, or any kind of public accommodation. Public manners are good, brawls and disturbances are rare, and private attachments are often strong and affectionate. Intermarriage is common, but because there is in an important sense no such thing as an Anglo-Afrikaner culture, children, but especially grandchildren, tend to revert to one of the original cultures. The ordinary radio services are distinct, but the commercial service is extraordinarily enterprising in its use of both languages, and many English-speaking people keenly enjoy Afrikaans humor.

In sports, the Afrikaner has not only taken over the English game of rugby football, but has made himself one of the world's greatest exponents of it. He plays tennis, and to a lesser extent cricket. If he has a national game, it is rugby football. The game of jukskei, portrayed by Mr. Weiner, is a cultural phenomenon and a social occasion as well as a game, an assertion of individuality, not likely to emerge as a serious competitor with other national games.

Politically, the two races have never been more divided than today. And, as everyone knows, politics penetrate every area of life. In South Africa the tendency has been—admirably so—for things like football to be kept out of politics; yet even that has proved difficult at times.

The problem of the multi-racial country is tough and complex. Our present Government's political solution is one of separate development for all races, under the rule of Afrikaner Nationalism. Many of us do not think it can last, yet at the moment the Government is in an apparently impregnable situation. Politics aside, the story of the Afrikaner is one of the most fascinating in the world.

38

38. This is the Little Karroo, as seen from the top of the Zwartberg. The Zwartberg Pass connects the Little with the Great Karroo. The traveller approaching from the Great Karroo will search the towering wall in vain for any way to ascend it. Of its kind, the Pass is the most magnificent in South Africa, harsh, somber and austere.

39. An African woman and child are travelling in the Great Karroo. Her husband is a farm laborer, and she is transporting their household possessions to new employment. The plain here is dry, flat and monotonous, but in the far distance can be seen the Zwartberg, the Black Mountain.

40

40. Storm over the Great Karroo. When rain comes to these arid regions, the change is miraculous. In Namaqualand, the whole land bursts into flower: the dimorphotheca, the Aus daisy, the arctotis, and the other desert ephemerals, together with mesembryanthemums of every size, habit and hue.

41. A Dutch Reformed church on the Little Karroo. The Church plays a tremendous role in Afrikaner life, and has always been closely identified with the struggles and aspirations, social, political, cultural, educational, and economic, of the Afrikaner people.

42

42 & 43. A respected Afrikaner farmer of the Orange Free State.

43

44. The farmer visits the house of one of his laborers, and gives instructions for the next day's work.

45. The massive Voortrekker Monument, situated on a hill outside Pretoria. It is the national shrine of the Afrikaner people, and annually on the Day of the Covenant, December 16, it is the scene of great religious and patriotic gatherings.

45

46. Statue of Paul Kruger, President of the Transvaal Republic at the time of the Anglo-Boer War of 1899. The President died in Switzerland, but today his old Republic rules South Africa.

46

47. Part of the Vroue-monument in Bloemfontein, commemorating the death of over 20,000 women and children in the concentration camps set up by the British. An Englishwoman, Emily Hobhouse, who did much to improve conditions in the camps, is honored here. The Vroue-monument commemorates one of the most tragic events in the whole history of South Africa, and is an austere and moving memorial in somber stone.

48

49

50

51

48, 49, 50 & 51. The national Afrikaner game of jukskei, as played in the capital city of Pretoria. This is more than a game, it is also an assertion of individuality, and a social and cultural occasion.

JOHANNESBURG

WHEN I was a boy I found it, as I find it today, exciting to approach Johannesburg. It is our Big City; it enables us to boast to the outside world, much of which believes we live in a kind of jungle, that we know what a big city is.

Johannesburg came into being in 1886, a rowdy collection of huts and tents, disturbing the pastoral peace of a republic that desired nothing more than to be left alone. One can imagine how warily Pretoria eyed the upstart city, situated only 36 miles away.

But Johannesburg did more than bring the British to the Transvaal, it did more even than evoke those passions which ultimately led to the Anglo-Boer War. It began to destroy the foundations of the tribal system, and it began—though not with intention —to challenge the whole notion of *apartheid* in a modern industrial society.

Consider for a moment the old republics. They were pastoral states. On the whole the trekkers had not found it difficult to conquer the people of the African tribes. Reserves had been set aside for them under the authority of their chiefs. Displaced black people, of which there were many during those turbulent times, settled on the white men's farms, and so achieved security and other benefits in return for their labor. Thus there could be said to be two kinds of African people, the tribesman and the farm laborer.

But a small third class was already emerging, and these were the town dwellers. They were not numerous, because the towns were few in number and small in size. They had been established as republican capitals, market places, church centers, and even as refuges in case of trouble with the tribes. In these small places the white householders wanted a servant, the white blacksmith wanted a bellows boy, the white shopkeeper wanted a carrier to send out with the goods. A separate portion of the town, called the "location", was set apart for them to live in.

With the founding of Johannesburg, and the springing up of the smaller mining towns, the African urban class began to grow apace. These urban dwellers were for the most part not miners at all; they were quite distinct from the mine laborers, who, leaving their wives and children in the reserves, came and lived under strict supervision in the mine compounds. These urban dwellers were rather the workers without whom the life of a modern city cannot go on. They formed a new kind of African society altogether, a modern urban society, which is still in painful process of achieving itself.

The Nationalist Government takes the view that the African town dweller, when he chooses to make his home and seek his livelihood in the white man's city, must recognize that he cannot expect to participate in the rights and responsibilities of the city community. In his own "locations" he may enjoy certain local rights, but he cannot expect to have any say in city government, nor in the government of the country.

The continuous stream of Africans to the cities created tremendous problems, notably in the field of housing. Workers and work-seekers choked up the "locations"; they spilled over into the shanty-towns, preserving in all this squalor an incredible lustiness of life, and often a high standard of conduct. But they suffered casualties enough in broken homes, drunkenness, prostitution, high illegitimacy, crime and delinquency. Neglected youths became dangerous ones, and sent white people to gunsmiths, locksmiths, and psychiatrists.

Johannesburg is today a city of a million people, but it does not stop growing. It is the central town of the Witwatersrand, which is a long string of mining towns, Germiston, Boksburg, Benoni, Springs, and Nigel on the East Rand; Roodepoort, Maraisburg, Krugersdorp and Randfontein on the West. But the Golden Reef does not stop there; it stretches further west than that, and turning south, crops up again in the Orange Free State, richer than ever. There another string of towns is growing up, with the promise of equalling the Witwatersrand in mining importance though not in population.

Johannesburg is the terminal of several world airlines, as well as the most important center of the South African Airways, which itself maintains a regular service to London. The traveller who comes to South Africa by air will land at the modern airport of Jan Smuts, named after the second Prime Minister of the Union of South Africa. If he arrives by night after the long journey over what appears to be almost an empty continent, the sight of the lights of Johannesburg will be astonishing. The city itself is modern, and has an appearance more American than European. If the traveller visits every part of it, he cannot but be struck by the extremes of wealth and poverty, nor can it escape his notice that wealth is white and poverty is black.

This great disparity is to be explained in two ways. In the first place it is the inevitable accompaniment of the whole process of industrialization and urbanization, and of the profound change that has come over African life with the coming of the white man; industry wants labor, and is not directly concerned with housing. Housing is the task of municipal authorities, whose record is sometimes good, sometimes bad. The disparity of wealth is also due to the color bar, which in many cases prevents—by law—Africans from doing work they are capable of doing. It is a mechanism of fear and selfishness, and its consequences are unforgivable. One must place on record here that while industry has maintained a color bar, it is also industry—new and expanding industry—that has given new opportunity and hope to African workers.

Yet industrialization and urbanization, and therefore material progress, are really contrary to the spirit of *apartheid*. There is a struggle here between economics and political ideology. Or, to put it in other words, Johannesburg and Pretoria are still at war.

52

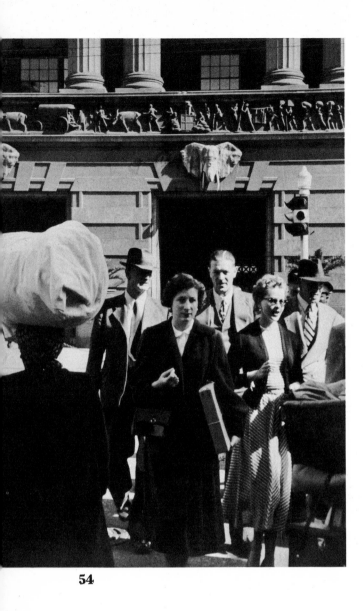

54

56. The beautiful grounds of Zoo Lake, Johannesburg. This magnificent park provides a fascinating study in South African customs. Though the various public facilities are allotted racially, there is no color bar in the grounds themselves. A young colored girl will be seen occupying one of the benches. To South Africans not familiar with Zoo Lake, the sight of this young girl causes a start, whether visible or not, of surprise. Some will find her presence intolerable, some distasteful, some a matter of indifference, some a cause for thankfulness.

54. The Entrance to the Johannesburg Railway Station, the most modern in Africa. The figures on the sculptured frieze are truly indigenous.

55. An African bus queue. This picture was taken at 7:00 p.m., and many of these people will not be home before 8:00 or 9:00 p.m. Yet they must rise again at 6:00 a.m. Bus transportation is a problem in South Africa because wages are low. Therefore fares must be low and the service is poor.

55

57

58

59

60

60. In 1955 the Government ordered and commenced the evacuation of Sophiatown, a non-white township, which though originally on the edge of Johannesburg, has since been encircled by white suburbs. Many of the properties were squalid in the extreme, and their occupiers will benefit from their transfer to the new "location" of Meadowlands; but some of the properties were held by Africans in freehold, and this right has been taken away. It is the intention of the Government to allow no African to own land outside the reserves, which constitute roughly ⅙ of the land area of the Union. While very many Africans welcomed the removal, the more politically conscious saw in it an invasion of personal rights. Hence the slogan "Defend Homes".

Here follow three examples of the kind of African housing which is due to be demolished or improved.

61. A shanty in Sophiatown.

62. A lane in Moroka.

63. Woman grinding snuff in a street in the Breezeblocks, Orlando, Johannesburg. She still wears her tribal adornments.

THE GOLD MINES

WHILE the great gold mining industry is largely responsible for the development of South Africa, and therefore for the emergence of the African town dweller, its own African underground labor is not drawn from that class.

These workers come from the reserves of the Union itself, and from Basutoland, Bechuanaland, Swaziland, Rhodesia, Mozambique, Nyasaland, and Tanganyika. They are still tribal in their culture, and come from places less affected by European influence, but they have admitted goldmining into their tribal pattern. Some will come a dozen or more times to the mines during their lives, each time for a period of about a year.

They live in large compounds, and great attention is paid to their health and recreation. At the beginning of the century, for example, the death rate from disease was 30 in every thousand, but in 1952 it had declined to 2.07 per thousand. Their tribal dancing is encouraged, and it is one of the sights of a lifetime to see such a dance; the earth shakes with the stamp of warriors' feet, and the air trembles with fierce and barbaric song, like nothing else that you have ever heard.

Our gold mines produce nearly half of the gold of the world; they give direct employment to nearly half-a-million people; they were responsible, directly and indirectly, for tremendous industrial development; towns declined or prospered according to the state of the mines near them; the railways, the shipping companies, the aviation companies, all depend on the mines for a considerable percentage of their custom.

The industry is nevertheless passing through an anxious time. While every other commodity has risen steadily in price, the United States will not pay a higher price for gold. Faced by rising prices in every other direction, the gold mining industry has kept going only by the use of economy, and more and more efficient methods.

A second difficulty is that the very industrial development which the mines initiated, now competes for labor. Everywhere Africa is in transition, and our neighbouring countries will need their labor for themselves.

It has often been said that the gold industry was dying, that all mineral wealth comes to an end. Pessimists have said that ten years, twenty years, thirty years, would see the end of gold, and that grass would grow in the streets of Johannesburg.

But in 1946 great new gold fields were discovered in the Orange Free State; their wealth is computed to be as great as the wealth of the Witwatersrand. The technical

difficulties are expected to be greater owing to the depth of the deposits, but the gold content of the ore is generally higher.

And now uranium has been discovered to be a component of the gold-bearing ores. South Africa is at the moment one of the greatest producers of uranium also. Now we find ourselves endowed with a mineral which, far from being a doubtful asset, is bound up with the whole future of the human race.

66

65 & 66.   Scenes from the mines. In No. 66 are shown miners off duty, wearing the blankets of which they are so fond. In Basutoland in particular the blanket is widely worn, both by men and women, even during the worst heat of summer.

67 & 68. One of the problems confronting mine authorities is that of using up the surplus physical energy of their tremendous labor forces. It is fortunate indeed that the African people have such a deep love of song and dance, and this the authorities foster and encourage. Here are seen groups of miners preparing for the dance. On special occasions the proper dress is worn, and the spectator will see sights and hear sounds not soon to be forgotten.

69. At leisure in the compound, watching the dance.

POLITICAL AND RACIAL PROBLEMS

THE problem of creating a society where different races may live together in peace appears to be extremely difficult. John Gunther in "Inside Africa", having regard to racial attitudes in South Africa, finds the problem insoluble under present circumstances. The present Nationalist Government sees the solution rather in the creation of separate sub-societies, under the rule and direction of itself. The Opposition, called the United Party, sees it in a society where men and women do the work of production and manufacture together, but otherwise remain separate; this leaves unanswered certain important political questions. Yet others, Liberals, see the solution in a common society, whose rights and responsibilities are shared by all. Each of these solutions appears to Gunther at present to encounter insuperable obstacles.

There is of course also the Communist solution, which could be expected to win increasing support in a country where there is such disparity of wealth. It is of this solution that the Government is most afraid, and it has taken severe action against the Communists. But it could not be maintained in 1956 that Communism is an important force; the most important reason for this is that the African people are as yet, from the standpoint of western democracy, politically unawakened, the second is that many of them are concerned with seizing the opportunities offered by the new way of life, higher wages, better houses, and better education for their children. Yet if the amount of frustration were to increase, there is no doubt that the Communist cause would be advanced.

There is a fifth political power, that of African Nationalism. If it should become the instrument of vengeance, whether allied to Communism or not, then we may with Mr. Gunther look forward with little hope. If it should become, as it professedly desires, the champion of a wider democracy, anything might happen.

The fact is that South Africa is full of virile peoples. They have each made their contribution to the present wealth and increasing importance of the country. One thing seems clear, that ultimately no political solution of the problem can endure unless it has the support of the politically unawakened and politically awaking African people. We would be foolish to expect that this support will be given to any solution which

seems to them to detract from their dignity as human beings. If I know or understand anything of the African people, it is that they have a fierce hunger to be recognized by the people of the world as their fellows and equals. When I look at the magnificent picture with which this book concludes, I am confirmed in my belief that this will be so.

71 & 72. Both of these pictures are very meaningful. In the one is depicted an African clergyman and his wife, upholders of the religion which the white man brought to Africa. It would be foolish to suppose that the adoption of Christianity by the African people is a mere empty aping of Western custom. On the contrary, their humble devotion restores to Western Christianity an essential element that has been lost. In the other picture, an African woman, with her child on her back, looks into a modern shop window. I cannot describe the expression on her face, because it is indescribable.

73

73, 74 & 75. These are unusual pictures. They show white and non-white people together at what appears to be some kind of social gathering. Where could this be? It could be at several, but few, places. This happens to be a mission station in Johannesburg. The Government has recently passed the Bantu Education Act, which will have the effect of removing control of African education from missionary bodies, and placing it under the control of the State. If you have read the brief history at the beginning of this book, you will better understand the reason for this.

74

75

76.   To be, but what to be, that is the question.

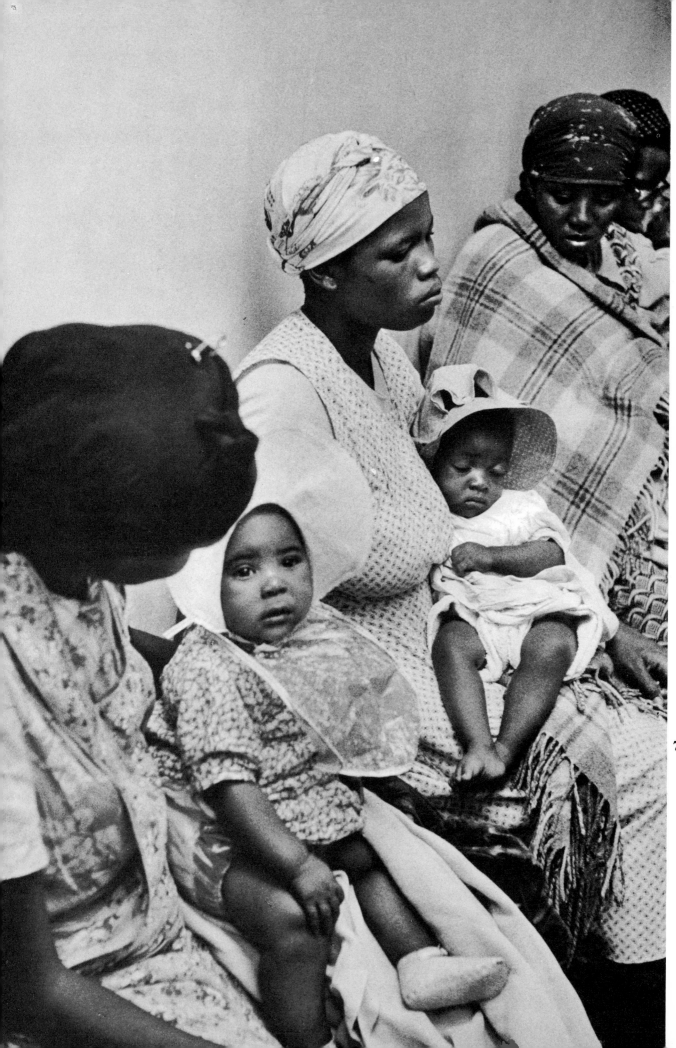

77 & 78. It is pleasing to record the increasing trust that African people have come to place in Western medicine, and in Western hospitals, doctors, and nurses. Increasing numbers of African and Indian girls are being drawn into the profession of nursing.

80

81

79. An African welder for whom the Industrial Revolution has opened what would have remained a forbidden door.

80. An African schoolmistress supervising a school meal in Johannesburg.

81. Four young African women of the new generation.